QEB
START
Reading

Children Around the World

Verna Wilkins

QEB Publishing, Inc.

QEB

Published in the United States by
QEB Publishing, Inc.
23062 La Cadena Drive
Laguna Hills, CA 92653
www.qeb-publishing.com

Library of Congress Control Number 2004101901

ISBN 1-59566-138-7

Written by Verna Wilkins
Designed by Zeta Jones
Editor Hannah Ray
Picture Researcher Joanne Beardwell

Series Consultant Anne Faundez
Creative Director Louise Morley
Editorial Manager Jean Coppendale

Printed and bound in China

Picture credits

Key: t = top, b = bottom, m = middle, c = center, l = left, r = right

Corbis/Anthony Bannister 14tr, /Owen Franken 10tc, /So Hing-Keung 6-7,
/Wolfgang Kaehler 10–11, /David Katzenstein 12–13, /Earl & Nazima Kowall 13t,
/Jacques Langevin 20–21, /Lawrence Manning 17t, /Stephanie Maze 16–17, /Paul A
Souders 14–15, /Tom Stewart 21bl, /Staffan Widstrand 8–9; **Trip**/Helene Rogers 4–5,
18–19.

Contents

Great Britain

"I am Janet. My best friend is Kim. We both live in London, in England.

We walk together to our big, new school. We love recess.

My favorite food is pizza.

My favorite game is soccer."

United States

"I am Amy. I live in New York City. New York is full of tall buildings called skyscrapers.

I love baseball. My favorite team is the Yankees. I play Little League baseball every Saturday.

My mom is a doctor. Dad is a teacher."

Canada

"My name is Kipanik. I live near Iqaluit, in northern Canada.

I go to school in a **snowmobile**. When my dad was little, he rode a dog sled.

I love stories about long ago.

I like making snowmen as big as me!"

Brazil

"My name is Davi. My home is near a river in the rainforest. At night, I sleep in a **hammock**, which hangs from the ceiling.

I swim in the river with my two older sisters and brother. They never let me swim alone. There are alligators in the river."

11

India

ST. PAUL'S SCHOOL
Vempeer Nagar/Chandra Puri, Mathura.
NURSERY TO XII

"I am Kamal. I can speak Hindi and English. Lila is my little sister.

My father drives me to school in his taxi. Writing stories is my favorite subject at school."

Africa

"Jambo! That means 'hello' in Swahili, my language. I am Asha. I live in Kenya.

Dad takes visitors to see the lions, zebra, cheetahs, and elephants that live near my home.

When I grow up, I want to write books about animals."

China

"I am Lin. I live in Beijing.

I like going to school with my friends.

At home, I love watching cartoons on TV.

My little sister is learning to eat with chopsticks."

Australia

"I am named Alice, after the Outback town Alice Springs. My mother was born there. My father was born in England. We live near Perth, in Western Australia.

I have just learned to swim and ride my bike. We often have **barbecues**.

I've seen lots of kangaroos and koalas. My favorite animal is the koala bear."

19

Caribbean

"I am Lola. My school is near the beach, in St. Lucia. This is a hot country. Sometimes we have classes outside.

I love to play **hopscotch** and jump-rope in the playground.

My dad is a fireman. My mom is a teacher. I have one older brother. His name is Levi.

My favorite food is rice and peas."

Glossary

 **barbecue**—cooking food outside using burning charcoal or a gas grill.

 **hammock**—a piece of cloth that is hung above the ground and used to rest or sleep in.

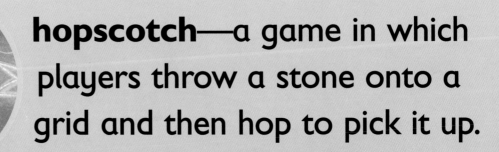 **hopscotch**—a game in which players throw a stone onto a grid and then hop to pick it up.

snowmobile—a special vehicle for traveling over snow.